HOW TO BE
SUCCESSFUL
WITHOUT HURTING
MEN'S

FEELINGS

What's the worst part of being a woman in business?

We asked these three men what they think.

HOW TO BE
SUCCESSFUL
WITHOUT HURTING
MEN'S
FEELINGS

NON-THREATENING LEADERSHIP STRATEGIES FOR WOMEN

—— SARAH COOPER ——

Andrews McMeel
PUBLISHING®

INTRODUCTION 1
No Feelings Were Harmed While Writing This Book

1: DREAMS. 7
How to Ace Your Job Interview Without Over-acing It

2: COMMUNICATION 23
How to Talk Like a Man but Still Be Seen as a Woman

3: AMBITION 41
How to Advance Your Career Without Shoving It
in Everyone's Face

4: AUTHENTICITY. 59
How to Bring Your True Self to Work and Then
Hide It Completely

5: DIVERSITY 75
An Honest Look at Diversity in the Tech Industry

6: LEADERSHIP 89
Non-threatening Leadership Strategies for Women

BREAK. 105
A Few Blank Pages to Doodle on When Men Are
Explaining Things

TABLE OF

CONTENTS

7: NEGOTIATION 113
Gaslighting for Beginners

8: HARASSMENT 127
How to Be Harassed Without Hurting His Career

9: SUCCESS 145
Choose Your Own Adventure: Do You Want to Be
Likeable or Successful?

10: ALLIES 159
Men's Achievement Stickers

11: ENTREPRENEURSHIP 173
The Perfect Pitch Deck for the Kickass Lady Boss

12: SELF-CARE 189
How to Relax While Still Completely Stressing
Yourself Out

CONCLUSION 205
Be Threatening

SPECIAL THANKS 208

No Feelings Were Harmed While Writing This Book

When I started to write *How to Be Successful Without Hurting Men's Feelings*, my biggest fear was that my book would be successful and hurt men's feelings. After all, that was the last thing I wanted to do.

You see, every morning I wake up and ask myself the same question: How dare I?

How dare I seek opportunities? How dare I speak up? How dare I know stuff? How dare I tell a man he's wrong? How dare I tell a man he's right? He's a man! He knows he's right!

Asking myself these questions every day has given me the strength I need to take all my hopes and dreams and push them deep, deep down inside where they can only be seen in the glimmer of my eye when I get too angry to talk.

But sometimes that glimmer is too bright and that's not good either. Because you know what's more precious than my hopes and dreams? A man's ego.

A man's ego must be protected at all cost.

But Sarah, you ask, what if a man is about to make a horrible mistake, one that could kill him? Shouldn't I interject then?

No. You shouldn't.

Take the story of Mary. One evening, Mary was riding in a car with her coworker, Steve, on their way to a company offsite. It was early evening and Steve had forgotten to turn on his headlights. Mary kindly said, "Your lights aren't on." Steve laughed slightly and turned them on. Mary was relieved that Steve was such a good sport about it and they went on to have a very pleasant and expectedly useless team bonding experience.

The ride home was not as easy.

Driving back, Steve made the same mistake and forgot to turn his headlights on. This time, Mary hesitated before correcting him, especially since there were other coworkers in the car this time. But after a few seconds of thought she figured correcting him was the safest thing to do for everyone involved. I'm sure you can imagine what happened next. Mary told Steve to turn on his headlights, the coworkers in the backseat laughed at Steve's mistake, Steve became flustered, embarrassed and momentarily blinded by rage, ran a stop sign, and T-boned an SUV. Fortunately, everyone survived. Unfortunately, everyone blamed Mary for causing the accident.

Coworkers taunted her for trying to tell Steve how to drive. Mary tried to defend herself by insisting she did the right thing.

But Mary did the wrong thing. The very wrong thing.

If you have the choice between saving a man's ego or saving his life, trust me. Save his ego. He'll thank you for it later. I mean, he won't because he'll be dead, but you know what I mean.

When you hurt a man's ego it's as painful as death anyway. Forgetting to turn his headlights on is just a less extreme example of soul-crushing workplace mistakes such as putting the wrong date on a presentation, leaving a zero off of an estimate, making the wrong bet on the future of the company's product line, or sleeping with an intern and costing the company millions of dollars in lawsuits.

As women, we might be tempted to say, "Excuse me, you made a small error here." DO NOT SAY THIS. As non-threatening women, we must avoid that instinct because it serves no one, least of all ourselves.

Sadly, this isn't just about pointing out mistakes. It's about commanding any kind of presence at work. Being ambitious, seeking power, showing knowledge, these are all dangerous paths if we really want to be successful and get ahead.

As a woman in the business world, I kept seeing other women make the same mistakes over and over again. Telling their coworkers they wanted to be promoted. Asking their managers for more money. Bringing visibility to their work, leading meetings, talking in meetings, looking around in meetings, and breathing in meetings.

Seeing this, I knew my calling was to write a book that would stop the frustration born out of making an effort. I learned many of these tips while I was working in the male-dominated world of tech. Although I still messed up and was threatening every once in a while, I generally held fast to these rules and they probably definitely helped me get somewhere, I think.

How to Be Successful Without Hurting Men's Feelings is the non-threatening leadership guide women must follow if we are to be taken seriously in the workplace. And by "seriously," of course, I mean "not seriously," which is how we should always strive to be taken. And by "strive," of course, I mean "accept."

This book covers everything from how to land that dream job by not dreaming too big to how to deal with harassment while protecting your harasser, as well as pages for doodling on when men are talking at you and you need to be patient and let them finish what they're saying.

Each chapter also includes an exercise designed to challenge you to be less challenging. I like to call these my "inaction items."

Because sometimes doing nothing is the best something we can not do.

So arm yourself with the knowledge of these pages, ladies. Be vigilant about hiding yourself. (Not your entire self, just the woman and/or minority part of yourself.)

Scale the heights of your career and break that glass ceiling, but do it very quietly and gingerly, and be sure to make a man think he did it for you.

By standing as still as possible, you will go farther than you ever imagined, as long as you didn't imagine going too far.

I AM

Woman

→ HEAR ME ←

ROAR

Very Softly

SO AS NOT TO STARTLE ANYONE

How to Ace Your Job Interview Without Over-acing It

In today's competitive job market, it's important for women to be very careful about how they present themselves. We have to be friendly, but not too friendly; awesome, but not too awesome; and completely comfortable in our own skin as long as we fit right in.

Oftentimes following all the rules seems impossible, and that's because it is.

Here are a few rules to keep in mind if you want to nail your next job interview.

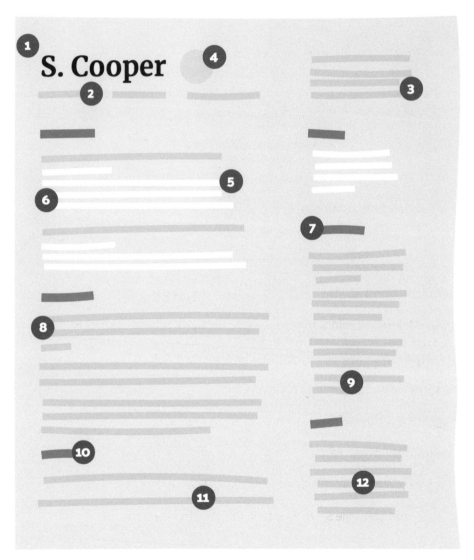

S. Cooper

Gender-neutralize your resume

Make sure your resume doesn't scream "female" by following these gender-neutral resume guidelines:

1. Use initials instead of your full first name

2. Avoid all pronouns in your professional summary

3. Use a male-sounding email address, such as "yeahboy23@gmail.com"

4. Replace your picture with an anime character

5. Sprinkle words like "gamechanger" throughout

6. For bullet points, use the male symbol

7. Use only the color blue to suggest color blindness

8. Use incomplete sentences

9. Put "Male references available upon request"

10. Spell "skillz" with a z

11. List your favorite whiskey, scotch, or IPA

12. Add "X-Treme Sports" to your extracurricular interests

When to wear your wedding ring

PHONE INTERVIEW

IN-PERSON INTERVIEW

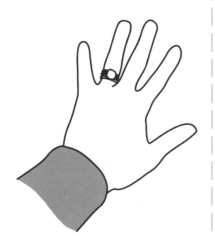

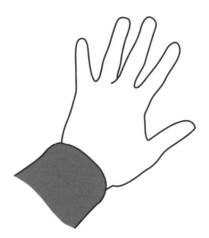

If you're married, feel free to wear your wedding ring during your phone interview but take it off when interviewing in person. This will help you achieve that "I won't be getting pregnant soon" look. When you get the job, make sure to hide your married status at least until after your first promotion.

How much to smile

TOO FLIRTY

TOO BITCHY

JUST RIGHT

How much should you smile during your job interview? The answer is: not too much and definitely not too little. Try practicing a smile that's somewhere in between, even if it makes you look like you're having a stroke. This is your best option.

Hairstyles to avoid

TOO SEXY

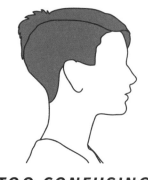

TOO CONFUSING

TOO LAZY

TOO RELIGIONY

Here's a handy diagram of hairstyles to avoid so you can make the best first impression.

TOO BORING

TOO OLD

TOO BLACK

WAY TOO BLACK

TOO CASUAL

TOO DISTRACTING

TOO STUFFY

PERFECT

What not to wear

Here's a list of clothing options to avoid when trying to nail that big interview:

- See-through blouses
- V-neck blouses
- Scoop-neck blouses
- Blouses
- Tight-fitting dresses
- Loose-fitting dresses
- Short skirts
- Shorts
- Jeans
- Jean shorts
- Leggings
- Jeggings
- Heavy jackets
- Flower patterns
- Unflattering stripes or polka-dot patterns
- Bold colors
- Muted colors
- Exposed tattoos
- Hidden tattoos
- Yoga pants
- Tight slacks
- Thigh-high boots
- Thigh-high socks
- Open-toe heels
- Sneakers
- Festive nails
- Activist t-shirts
- Band t-shirts
- Fringe
- Lots of accessories
- Lack of accessories
- Hats
- Scarves
- Bow ties
- Tank tops
- Sweaters
- Turtlenecks
- Button-downs
- Button-ups

Voice loudness

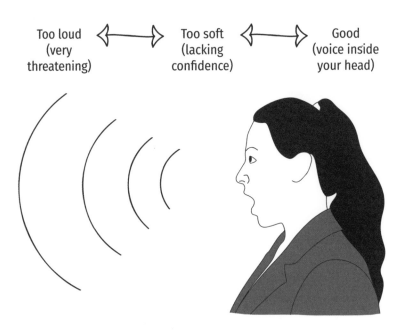

Too loud
(very
threatening)
⟨⟶⟩
Too soft
(lacking
confidence)
⟨⟶⟩
Good
(voice inside
your head)

When speaking during your interview, it's important to speak passionately but not so loud that you scare your interviewers. You also don't want to speak too softly, either. However, speaking to yourself, in your head, is always permitted, especially if it's to remind yourself to not speak too much.

≥ Voice pitch ≤

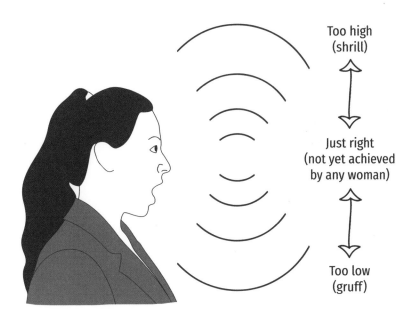

Too high
(shrill)

Just right
(not yet achieved
by any woman)

Too low
(gruff)

Voice pitch is very tricky for women. Our normal speaking voices are naturally shrill and annoying, or too deep and not feminine enough. We must practice constantly to speak in a tone that's pleasing to the male ear. In fact, we may be practicing for the rest of our lives because this tone has not yet been discovered.

Taking credit

"ARROGANT"   **NOT QUALIFIED**

This project was very successful and I owned it start to finish

You know, it was really a team effort

When describing your accomplishments, you need to strike a balance between tooting your own horn and hiding your horn behind the shed. This is difficult because if you don't take enough credit you won't seem qualified, but if you take too much credit you'll seem arrogant. Good luck with that.

Negotiation

"INTIMIDATING"

Can we discuss salary?

DOESN'T VALUE HERSELF

Sounds great, I'll take it

Never accept a position without negotiating your salary. However, when asking to negotiate you might come off as demanding. But if you don't negotiate, people will think you don't value yourself. So, feel your new employer out. Ask them what they'd do in your situation. Or, don't do that. It's really a no-win situation anyway.

Conclusion

When it comes to landing a new job, it's easy to let all the contradictory advice confuse you, leaving you feeling paralyzed. But you can't let that happen, because you are a strong woman and the power is in your hands. However, if you come across as too strong and too powerful, well, you might end up empty-handed.

You need to let things happen naturally. So ignore the advice, but also follow it, but also think for yourself. It's all about finding that perfect balance that doesn't exist.

EXERCISE: LOW EXPECTATIONS

One thing I often ask myself is, how can I keep my career expectations as low as possible so that I won't be disappointed?

Use this worksheet to think about what you truly want for your life, your family, and your career, then how you can lower those desires and expect much less.

LOW EXPECTATIONS

ACTION PLAN

MY DREAM	MY LOWER EXPECTATION
FAMILY	
A supportive husband and one or two kids	Enough money to freeze my eggs in time
LIFE	
CAREER	

ARE YOU *Overthinking* EVERYTHING? MAYBE YOU ARE *but maybe you're not?*

How to Talk Like a Man but Still Be Seen as a Woman

In male-dominated workplaces, women must join The Boys Club. That means acting more like men and less like women.

However, sometimes when women say the exact same thing a man says it's interpreted in a completely different way. It's enough to make you want to cry (which as a man means you're sensitive and as a woman means you're hysterical).

Here are a few phrases to completely avoid as a woman in the working world.

HELPFUL   ABRASIVE

DISRUPTOR | DISRUPTIVE

This really pisses me off

PASSIONATE

EMOTIONAL

CONFIDENT

ARROGANT

DETAIL ORIENTED

SLOW

FAMILY ORIENTED

IRRESPONSIBLE

FOCUSED

A BITCH

BUSY

NOT A TEAM PLAYER

HAS AMBITION

HAS AN ATTITUDE

HE NEEDS ANOTHER CHANCE

SHE NEEDS ANOTHER JOB

Conclusion

Some might say that how other people interpret your words is their problem, which is true. But it's also your problem because getting ahead in your career is all about soft skills. But for women, our soft skills can't be too soft and we can't just depend on our hard skills to do the work for us.

So what am I saying here? I have no idea. I'm just talking circles at this point, and that's okay because I'm doing it in a very, very soothing tone.

EXERCISE: POLICE YOUR OWN TONE

Tone policing is an insidious way for people to disregard what you are saying by adjusting the focus to how you're saying it. Since this is bound to happen to you at some point, it's best to start policing your own tone so others don't have to do it for you.

Use this worksheet to match what you're saying to how you should be saying it.

POLICE YOUR OWN TONE

WORKSHEET

Asking a question	Whisper
Giving a presentation	Monotone
Saying you're running late	Sing-song
Complaining	Upturn
Sharing your opinion	Apologetic
Expressing disapproval	Sultry
Giving feedback	Joking
Excusing yourself	Dying
Interviewing a candidate	Yellowish
Leading a meeting	Silent
Giving instructions	Mousy
Questioning the process	Wishy-washy
Asking for a raise	Tepid
Asking for a promotion	Wind
Leaving early	Saccharine

Bonus Tip

PREFERRED FORMS of WORKPLACE COMMUNICATION

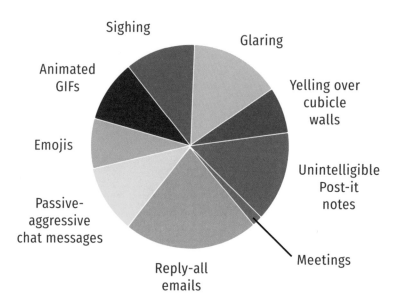

Bonus Tip

WHAT ARE WE DOING at WORK?

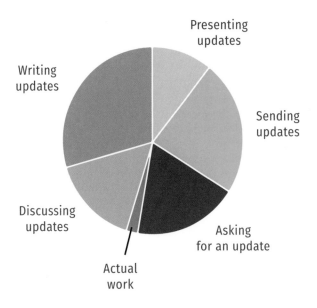

Presenting updates

Sending updates

Asking for an update

Actual work

Discussing updates

Writing updates

THE
Louder
YOU TYPE
THE
MORE
Productive
YOU LOOK

CHAPTER 3: AMBITION

How to Advance Your Career Without Shoving It in Everyone's Face

In the corporate world, men have perfected the art of office bullshit to make it seem like they're the hardest workers at the company, even when they haven't done any real work in years. You can use these same tactics to make sure everyone knows how dedicated you are without having to come out and say, "Hey everyone, look how dedicated I am," which, of course, would be career suicide.

Here are eleven subtle tricks that will give you the visibility you need while also keeping you as invisible as possible.

#1: Complain about how much email you get

Always complain about your email volume, but never be the first to say a specific number. I once complained because I had 200 unread emails and I was laughed out of the breakroom. Instead, find out how much email everyone else gets, and then double it. That's how much email you get.

#2: **Put several private events on your work calendar**

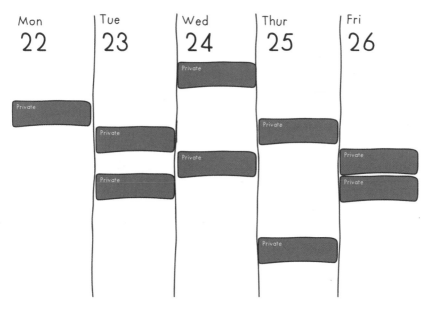

When a colleague checks out your work calendar and finds it brimming with private events, they'll immediately be impressed with how busy you are. Are you working on a secret project? Are you interviewing at another company? In their eyes, you'll now be viewed as a highly sought-after company resource, and they'll want a piece of the action.

#3: Leave your documents open all the time

Wow, Sarah is STILL reading the document, amazing

If you use Google Docs or any other real-time collaboration application, make sure it always appears as if you are active in the document, even when you're not. This will give you that coveted "constantly working" appearance, whether or not you are actually constantly working.

#4: **Always use a "Sent from my phone" email signature**

Use a "sent from my phone" signature, even when you're not sending from your phone. This makes you look like you're always busy and on the go, and also gets you out of proofreading.

#5: Share random thoughts at odd hours

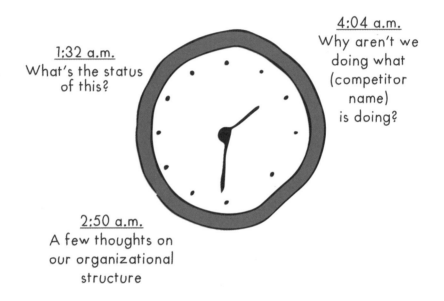

1:32 a.m.
What's the status of this?

4:04 a.m.
Why aren't we doing what (competitor name) is doing?

2:50 a.m.
A few thoughts on our organizational structure

Send emails on the weekend and in the middle of the night. You'll have folks wagging their tongues about how dedicated you are to be thinking about the company at 3 a.m.

#6: Send frequent updates about your whereabouts

I'm in a cab.

I'm going through security.

I'm at the gate but I'm about to go to the bathroom.

I'm in the bathroom.

I'm washing my hands.

I'm drying my hands.

It's important to let everyone know where you are at every moment—as well as the minute-to-minute status of your Internet access. Make sure your team knows there's a virtual umbilical cord between you and your work. This makes you seem like someone whose team really needs them at all times.

#7: Use math words to sound smart

One way to subtly sound smart in work conversations is to utilize math words. Here's a few you can use and how to use them:

EXPONENTIAL
Instead of: "Our soapless hand-washing app is experiencing massive growth."
Try: "We've got *exponential* growth."

ORTHOGONAL
Instead of: "Vegan lunches have nothing to do with getting more espresso machines."
Try: "That's an *orthogonal* issue."

DELTA
Instead of: "Both marketing proposals sound great, but what are the differences?"
Try: "What's the *delta* here?"

THIRD QUADRANT
Instead of: "There's nothing positive about this review we got on Bloomberg."
Try: "This is a *third quadrant* situation."

BINARY

Instead of: "Either you're going to give us a million dollars or you're not."
Try: "Look, it's a *binary* outcome."

HYPERBOLIC

Instead of: "Aren't you exaggerating?"
Try: "Aren't you being a bit *hyperbolic*?"

ASYMPTOTIC

Instead of: "We keep almost making money but we never quite get there."
Try: "We have *asymptotic* profit."

MULTIVARIATE

Instead of: "We should a/b test these designs."
Try: "Let's do a *multivariate* test."

EXTRAPOLATE

Instead of: "Based on March numbers, April will be bad."
Try: "I was able to *extrapolate* when we're going to run out of money."

NULL

Instead of: "We can't afford to pay you this quarter."
Try: "Your salary is *null*."

#8: Walk around with your laptop open

Walking around with your laptop open is a great way to show everyone at the office that you don't waste any time. It also makes you look like you're too busy for a quick chat right now.

#9: When writing an email, use as many acronyms as possible

The use of acronyms shows how you've mastered your company's shorthand. Even better, if someone doesn't know what an acronym means, it gives you a chance to explain it in a very condescending way. Start every email with a bullet point summary, labeled "TL;DR" (Too long; don't read).

#10: Always leave with your work bag

Always leave for the day with your laptop, work bag, and any extra papers and supplies you can find. Make sure people see that you're packing up your stuff to leave and go straight home to keep working, even if you plan on leaving it all in your car.

#11: Use an overly complex out-of-office responder

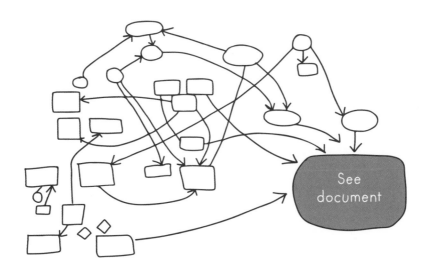

See document

If you're unable to respond to email for even just an hour, create an Out-of-Office (OOO) autoresponder that includes several people to get in touch with for each of your projects. For extra points, create an entire document that details everything you're working on and who to contact during your absence.

Conclusion

There's really no point to working your ass off if no one knows you're working your ass off, but be subtle about it. And when someone inevitably mentions all the hard work you've been putting in, it's important to act truly surprised, like you didn't even notice it. As women, it's important to work hard and appear passionate but also act like it's no big deal. This way, when you get a promotion, your boss will feel like he's rewarding your hard work when actually he's rewarding your lack of ambition. The less ambition you appear to have, the further you'll go.

EXERCISE: IMPOSTER SYNDROME CHECKLIST

Playing the game at work can be scary. You might feel like a fraud, like you're putting on a show, like you're not good enough. Luckily, feeling like a fraud is all part of the game. It's called "imposter syndrome" and all the best people have it. Do you have it? And is yours as good as everyone else's? Use this checklist to see how your imposter syndrome stacks up.

IMPOSTER SYNDROME

QUIZ

CHECK EACH STATEMENT THAT APPLIES TO YOU

- ☐ I don't deserve my success
2 POINTS

- ☐ What success? I've done nothing with my life
4 POINTS

- ☐ When someone criticizes me, I know they're right
2 POINTS

- ☐ When someone compliments me, I punch them in the neck
8 POINTS

- ☐ I am equally afraid to fail and afraid to succeed
4 POINTS

- ☐ I see all opportunities as a trap
6 POINTS

- ☐ Anything I accomplish is 90% luck and 10% luck
8 POINTS

30+ POINTS
I'd tell you how great your imposter syndrome is but I don't want you to punch me

20-29 POINTS
Your imposter syndrome is okay, not great, just okay, which is perfect really

19 POINTS OR LESS
You really need to work on your imposter syndrome, you believe in yourself too much

Bonus Tip

ANATOMY
of an EMAIL

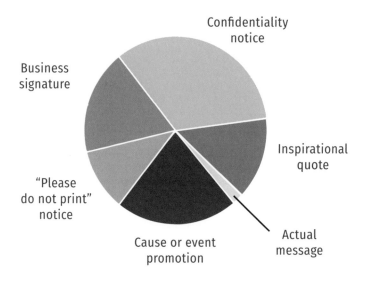

Confidentiality notice

Business signature

Inspirational quote

"Please do not print" notice

Actual message

Cause or event promotion

Bonus Tip

WHY I CC'ed YOU on this EMAIL

To guilt you into doing something

Because you're my boss and I want you to see I'm online

To prove later that you knew about this

To embarrass you for not doing something

As a power move

I thought it would be helpful

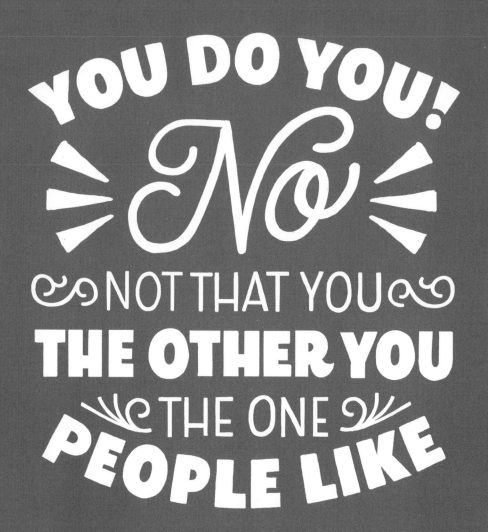

How to Bring Your True Self to Work and Then Hide It Completely

Authenticity is about bringing your whole self to work, except any part of you that makes you different in any way.

One common misconception about authenticity is that it means you need to be honest, when in fact it means you need to lie your ass off, for the greater good of your team and the company and the lesser good of yourself.

Here are a few pointers on striking the balance between honesty and authenticity.

Age

HONEST

Who's your favorite band?

Who's that?

Pearl Jam

"AUTHENTIC"

Who's your favorite band?

I dunno, who do you like?

Many people fall into the trap of being proud of their age. They share personal details which date them, such as pop culture, music, art, or literary references. This is a huge trap if you want to avoid ageism. Instead, limit your references to what the kids are talking about, and definitely don't listen to Pearl Jam* without headphones.

*Pearl Jam was an early '90s rock band

Family plans

HONEST

Do you plan to
have more kids?

I'm actually
pregnant now!

"AUTHENTIC"

Do you plan to
have more kids?

Oh God I can't
even think about
that right now!

Telling your coworkers about future family plans is risky. If they think
you'll be going on maternity leave soon, they could immediately start to
count you out for future projects. Try to keep your pregnancy a secret
until your child is at least eighteen years old.

Orientation

| HONEST | "AUTHENTIC" |

HONEST

Where's your wife?

My husband is a doctor, he's on call right now

"AUTHENTIC"

Where's your wife?

I'm flying solo tonight

If you aren't in a traditional relationship, better to keep that under wraps for as long as possible so you don't make your coworker feel awkward or yourself feel awkward having to answer their awkward questions about it.

Politics

Discussing politics at work is a huge no-no but there's bound to be someone who wants to talk about it, and that someone might be in charge of your paycheck. Keep your responses noncommittal and vague and save your screaming for later, when you can do it into your pillow.

Mental health

HONEST | **"AUTHENTIC"**

Why are you taking a leave of absence? Going somewhere fun?

Well, I suffer from depression...

Why are you taking a leave of absence? Going somewhere fun?

Maybe, we'll see

You may be bipolar, suffer from depression, or anxiety, or any number of other mental health issues. Your company absolutely supports you focusing on these issues and getting the help you need as long as it never comes up at work and you get all of your work done on time.

Blogging

HONEST	"AUTHENTIC"

What you do in your spare time is your business except if someone at work sees it, at which point it becomes everyone's business. If this happens, be sure to have a good way to play it off. Sure, softball or karaoke is fine, but doing anything that constitutes a full expression of your true self will get you fired.

Religion

HONEST	"AUTHENTIC"

Why aren't
you eating?

I'm observing
Ramadan

Why aren't
you eating?

I had a big
dinner

Religion at work is a tricky subject, especially if it affects your ability to join in team lunches, team-building offsites, or other outings. Although you might want to share your religion, especially if it's a big part of your life, it's best to minimize its importance so your coworkers don't think it will affect your ability to be a team player.

Addiction

HONEST	"AUTHENTIC"

| Why aren't you drinking? | I've been sober for 8 years | Why aren't you drinking? | Just don't feel like it |

Your sobriety is something to be proud of, except at work when everyone is drinking. You don't want to be left out when it's time to go for drinks, do you? So keep the option of having a drink in the future completely open, even if it's not even a remote possibility for you.

Confrontation

HONEST

"AUTHENTIC"

Happy to discuss this at any time

When all else fails and you can't hide from your coworkers emotionally, try hiding from them physically.

 # Being true to yourself

HONEST

I want to do
my own thing
here

"AUTHENTIC"

I'll do whatever everyone
else wants, I don't even
know who I am anymore

After years of hiding yourself, you'll eventually morph into your coworkers to the point where you are exactly like them. It is at this point you can be truly authentic since now you'll be a completely different person.

Conclusion

Authenticity is less about being the real you and more about finding someone successful to look up to and being that person instead. It's always a safe bet to simply mimic the actions, behaviors, clothes, thoughts, and feelings of the people at the top. Once you fully become those people, it'll be easy for other people to see you as someone who can move up in the company, too. However, if you do start to hide so much of yourself that you aren't really sure who you are anymore, you can always try regrounding yourself by spending time with your family.

EXERCISE: THE REAL ME

What do you wish your coworkers knew about you? What are some things you wish you didn't have to hide about yourself at work? Add these things to your vision board, then destroy this page.

THE REAL ME

VISION BOARD

ADD MAGAZINE CLIPPINGS, DRAWINGS, OR QUOTES HERE TO DESCRIBE THE REAL YOU, THEN RIP THIS PAGE UP SO NO ONE EVER SEES IT

Bonus Tip

HOW I SAY YES

I'd love to!

HOW I SAY NO

Sure.

Bonus Tip

THE MANY FACES *of a* PEOPLE PLEASER

Happy Bored Angry

Terrified Depressed Dying inside

"MAKE SURE THE *World* REMEMBERS YOUR NAME"

—Unknown

CHAPTER 5: DIVERSITY

An Honest Look at Diversity in the Tech Industry

In the interest of transparency (and in response to mounting pressure from the public), we are very excited to release our *Annual Diversity in Tech Report* and share all the gains we've made in hiring a wild array of different types of men.

Employee breakdown

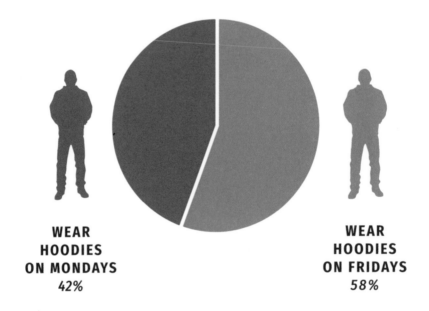

WEAR HOODIES ON MONDAYS
42%

WEAR HOODIES ON FRIDAYS
58%

When it comes to hoodies, our company hires a mix of people who wear hoodies on Mondays as well as Fridays and welcomes people from both orientations equally.

Employee breakdown

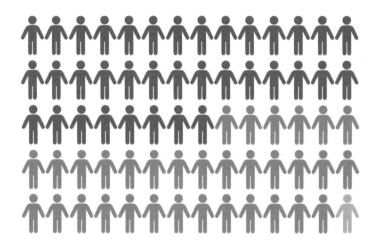

STANFORD CLASS OF '10 50%

STANFORD CLASS OF '11 48%

OTHER 2%

Our workforce is comprised of people from a wide span of graduating classes at Stanford.

Hiring criteria

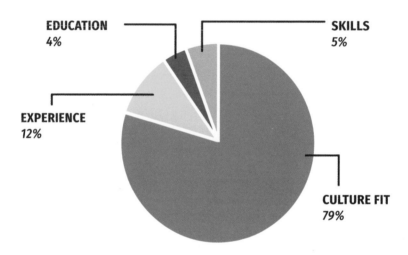

EDUCATION
4%

SKILLS
5%

EXPERIENCE
12%

CULTURE FIT
79%

When hiring, we look at a variety of factors, including education, experience, and skills. The biggest factor by far, though, is a candidate's ability to fit in with our existing culture. Some might say this is why we seem to only hire the same type of people, but who knows?

 Senior leadership

DRIVES A TESLA
35%

WANTS A TESLA
85%

TALKS ABOUT TESLA
99%

INVENTED TESLA
.034%

IS A TESLA
15%

Our standards for diversity extend to our senior leadership as well. At many companies, diversity weakens as you get to upper levels of leadership, but here we see even more diverse views of Tesla cars.

By role

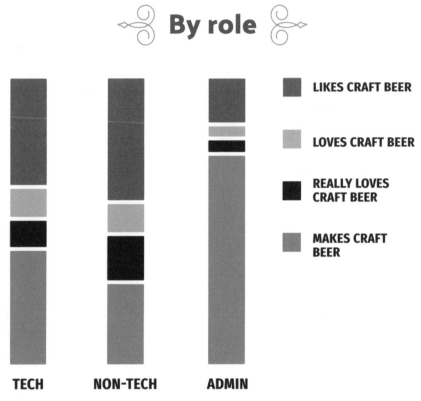

LIKES CRAFT BEER

LOVES CRAFT BEER

REALLY LOVES CRAFT BEER

MAKES CRAFT BEER

TECH   **NON-TECH**   **ADMIN**

Even by role, our company remains diverse, with a wide representation of people who like, love, really love, and make their own craft beer.

Sentiment

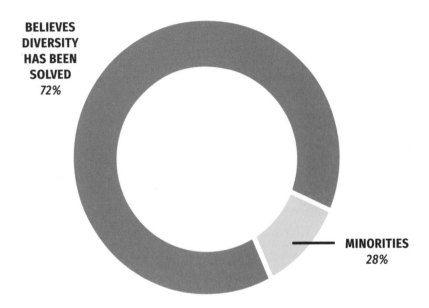

BELIEVES DIVERSITY HAS BEEN SOLVED
72%

MINORITIES
28%

When it comes to diversity, perception is as important as reality. As such, it is very heartening to us that most people feel like our problems with diversity have been largely solved.

Salaries

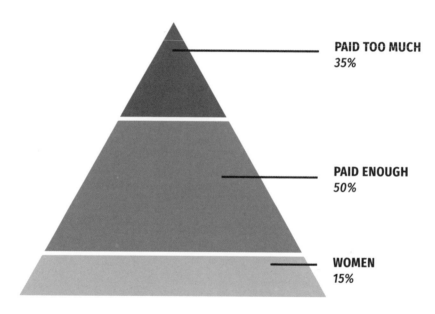

PAID TOO MUCH
35%

PAID ENOUGH
50%

WOMEN
15%

It's important that each one of our employees receives equal pay for equal work and that commitment is reflected in the wide representation of salaries across our company.

Inclusion

SPORTS ACTIVITIES
20%

DRINKING
20%

OTHER SPORTS ACTIVITIES
20%

MORE DRINKING
20%

MORE SPORTS ACTIVITIES
20%

EVEN MORE DRINKING
20%

Our employees enjoy a range of team-building activities to enrich our diverse culture.

Sexism

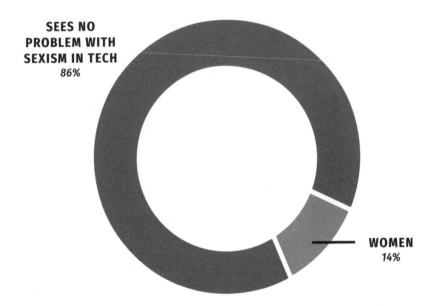

SEES NO PROBLEM WITH SEXISM IN TECH
86%

WOMEN
14%

Sexism in the technology industry is a huge problem, but it is encouraging to see that the vast majority of people don't experience it in their day-to-day lives.

Our Diversity Council

We continue to make diversity a top priority and have created a Diversity Council to lead and drive these efforts.

Conclusion

We are certainly thrilled with how far we've come in the past three months that we spent working on this diversity report. As you can see, we've made a lot of progress but still have a long way to go and we will certainly get there by the time our next report comes out. If you have any feedback or comments, please don't hesitate to reach out to us at [insert email address here].

EXERCISE: UNCONSCIOUS BIAS

Unconscious bias can affect all of us in different ways. Did you know that many men get judged based on their name alone? Test your unconscious bias in this worksheet by writing what kind of person you think would have each name.

UNCONSCIOUS BIAS

WORKSHEET

Chad

Bryce

Connor

Kyle

Hunter

Jaxon

Ethan

Zane

Logan

Tyler

Finn

Xander

Jared

Eugene

Tanner

Non-threatening Leadership Strategies for Women

In this fast-paced business world, female leaders need to make sure they're not perceived as pushy, aggressive, or competent. One way to do that is to alter your leadership style to account for the fragile male ego.

Should men accept powerful women and not feel threatened by them? Yes. Is that asking too much? IS IT? Sorry, I didn't mean to get aggressive there. Anyhoo, here are twelve non-threatening leadership strategies for women.

Setting a deadline

"THREATENING"

Get this done
by Monday

NON-THREATENING

What do you think
about getting this
done by Monday?

When setting a deadline, ask your coworker what he thinks of doing something, instead of just asking him to get it done. This makes him feel less like you're telling him what to do and more like you care about his opinions.

Sharing your ideas

"THREATENING"	NON-THREATENING
I have an idea	I'm just thinking out loud here

When sharing your ideas, overconfidence is a killer. You don't want your male coworkers to think you're getting all uppity. Instead, downplay your ideas as just "thinking out loud," "throwing something out there," or sharing something "dumb," "random," or "crazy."

Emailing a request

"THREATENING"

Send me the presentation when it's ready

NON-THREATENING

Hey Jake!! 😊 😊 Can I take a peek at your presentation when it's ready? Thanks!!! 😊 😊 😊

Pepper your emails with exclamation marks and emojis so you don't come across as too clear or direct. Your lack of efficient communication will make you seem more approachable.

Your idea is stolen

"THREATENING"	NON-THREATENING

That's exactly
what I just said

Thank you for
articulating
that so clearly

If a male coworker steals your idea in a meeting, thank him for it. Give him kudos for how he explained your idea so clearly. And let's face it, no one might've ever heard it if he hadn't repeated it.

Sexist comments

"THREATENING"	NON-THREATENING
That's not appropriate and I didn't appreciate it.	*awkward laugh*

When you hear a sexist comment, the awkward laugh is key. Practice your awkward laugh at home, with your friends and family, and in the mirror. Make sure you sound truly delighted even as your soul is dying inside.

 # You already knew that

"THREATENING"

I'm the one who taught you this six months ago

NON-THREATENING

I'd love for you to explain it to me

Men love explaining things. But when he's explaining something and you already know that, it might be tempting to say, "I already know that." Instead, have him explain it to you over and over again. It will make him feel useful and will give you some time to think about how to avoid him in the future.

Finding a mistake

"THREATENING"

These numbers
are wrong

NON-THREATENING

I'm sorry, are
these numbers
right? I'm not
100% sure,
I hate numbers

Pointing out a mistake is always risky so it's important to always apologize for noticing the mistake and then make sure that no one thinks you're too sure about it. People will appreciate your "hey what do I know?!" sensibilities.

Getting promoted

"THREATENING"	NON-THREATENING
I'd like to be considered for a promotion	I think you should consider Allison for a promotion

Asking your manager for a promotion could make you seem power-hungry, opportunistic, and transparent. Instead, ask a male coworker to vouch for you. Have your coworker tell your manager you'd be great for the role even though you don't really want it. This will make you more likely to actually get that promotion.

Getting ignored

"THREATENING"

Excuse me, can I introduce myself?

NON-THREATENING

Hey there!! ☺ ☺
I didn't get to
introduce myself
but I was in that
meeting earlier
today!!! ☺ ☺ ☺

Sometimes not everyone is properly introduced at the start of a meeting. Don't take it personally even if it happens to you all the time, and certainly don't stop the meeting from moving forward to introduce yourself. Sending a quick note afterward is the best way to introduce yourself without seeming too self-important.

Getting interrupted

"THREATENING"	NON-THREATENING

Can I finish
what I was
saying?

When you get interrupted, you might be tempted to just continue talking or even ask if you can finish what you were saying. This is treacherous territory. Instead, simply stop talking. The path of least resistance is silence.

Collaboration

"THREATENING"	**NON-THREATENING**
Type normally	Type using only one finger

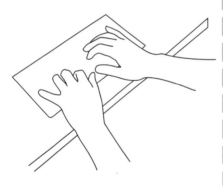 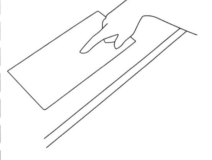

When collaborating with a man, type using only one finger. Skill and speed are very off-putting.

When you disagree

When all else fails, wear a mustache so everyone sees you as more man-like. This will cancel out any need to change your leadership style. In fact, you may even get a quick promotion!

Conclusion

Many women have discovered the secret power of non-threatening leadership. We call it a "secret power" because no one else actually knows about it. We keep our power hidden within ourselves so that it doesn't frighten and intimidate others. That's what makes us the true unsung heroes of the corporate world.

EXERCISE: WHAT I SHOULD'VE SAID

We all have times in our work life when we were way more threatening than we should've been. Think back to those times and think about what you should've said instead.

WHAT I SHOULD'VE SAID

WORSHEET

WHAT I SAID	WHAT I SHOULD'VE SAID
Actually, I can handle the presentation on my own	I would absolutely love your help, you know so much more than me

BREAK

A Few Blank Pages to Doodle on When Men Are Explaining Things

When men are talking, it's important to let them finish. Yes, even if you've already heard it, or what they're saying isn't relevant, or it's obvious no one is listening, or if they're explaining something they don't understand, or if they made their point twenty minutes ago and are now just saying the same thing over and over again using a different combination of words, etc.

To keep yourself preoccupied during these trying times, here are a few pages to doodle on.

WHATEVER YOU DO

Do it

with

Passion

OR WHATEVER

CHAPTER 7: NEGOTIATION

Gaslighting for Beginners

Gaslighting is a form of negotiation where people make you think you're crazy so you'll become confused and unsure of yourself and ultimately agree with whatever they're saying. You've definitely had it done to you, but you probably didn't even notice it. Oh, you did notice it? Are you sure? Do you even know what you're talking about? See, I just did it to you.

This top secret playbook is the same one all men receive when they start a new job. It will give you an inside look into how they use these tactics and how you can use them to your own advantage one day if you ever get the chance.

When asked a question, answer a related but much simpler question

Provide your non-answer in a very condescending tone, so your coworker feels like they just asked a very dumb question and will hesitate before asking you anything else.

If you're unfamiliar with a topic, dismiss it as not important

We need to identify our KPIs

We don't need to worry about that

Rather than admit you don't know something, simply say it's not relevant to the discussion, even if it's completely relevant to the discussion.

When giving instructions, be intentionally vague then blame the person for not understanding

Give instructions that are vague, out of order, and otherwise impossible to follow and never clarify them. When your coworker inevitably messes it up, blame them for not getting it right.

Look at your phone while your coworker is talking to you

Keep talking,
I'm just
multitasking

When a coworker starts talking, take out your phone and start browsing the Internet. Maybe laugh out loud a few times. This will make your coworker feel like what they're saying just isn't important.

When your coworker complains, bring up something else they really should be complaining about

I'm worried our quarterly planning sessions aren't working

What you really need to be worried about are the weekly reviews

When your coworker complains about something, bring up something completely unrelated that they should be complaining about. Then when what they were complaining about becomes a problem, ask them why they didn't bring it up sooner.

Say a question was already answered even though it wasn't

One of the easiest ways to make your coworker feel crazy is to pretend they aren't contributing anything new to the conversation and respond to everything they say as if it's already been covered.

Rephrase what people say into something completely different

> If we reverse the onboarding flow, we'll lose subscribers

> So you're saying we should reverse the onboarding flow

Rephrase what your coworker said but change the meaning completely. This will make them feel incapable of communicating clearly. When they try to correct you, suggest they take a communication class.

When someone shares a good idea, pretend like it sounds crazy then present it later as your own

We should redesign our ad system

That's insane. That would take forever

Maybe we should redesign our ad system

Always shoot down ideas privately as being ridiculous or too complicated, then present the same idea later as your own. If you're confronted about it, just say you didn't understand what they were saying and suggest they take a communication class.

Kill an idea, then when the project fails, ask why they didn't try that idea

So we're going to try this idea

That won't work, don't do that

You really should have tried that idea

The key to shooting down ideas is completely forgetting that you're the reason that idea got shot down. Remind your coworkers about the idea they should have tried as if it was 100% their fault they didn't try it. If they try to remind you that you shot it down, say they should've followed through if they really believed in it.

If you don't agree with an opinion, simply say no one has that opinion

If a coworker shares an opinion you don't agree with, invalidate it by saying no one has that opinion. Conversely, if someone disagrees with your opinion, say everybody shares your opinion. Point out the importance of not doing things based on what one person thinks (unless that person is you!).

Conclusion

One thing to keep in mind when being gaslighted is that the less you fight it and the sooner you accept it, the less crazy you will seem. At some point, you'll realize you're not crazy. Then you can point out that your question was valid or that everyone in the meeting was just as confused as you, but in a discreet way, like in an anonymous Hallmark card or scrawled in cream cheese on the gaslighter's bagel.

EXERCISE: GASLIGHTING DEFENSE

You may be confronted with self-affirming thoughts while being gaslighted. These thoughts will help you hold on to your sanity but should absolutely not be said out loud at the risk of becoming too threatening. Use this worksheet to append these thoughts with other thoughts that'll help you accept your gaslighting in silence.

GASLIGHTING DEFENSE

WORKSHEET

My opinion is valid   but I'll just keep it to myself

I have a right to ask this   but I'll ask someone else later

I'm not crazy   but I'll sound crazy if I keep talking

I'm not the only one who feels this way   but whatever

This makes no sense

I know what I'm talking about

People need to listen to me

I know I'm remembering this correctly

I'm not speaking another language

I know he heard me

I know I'm right

I know what I'm doing

I literally just said the answer

This is the wrong way to do it

What I'm saying makes sense

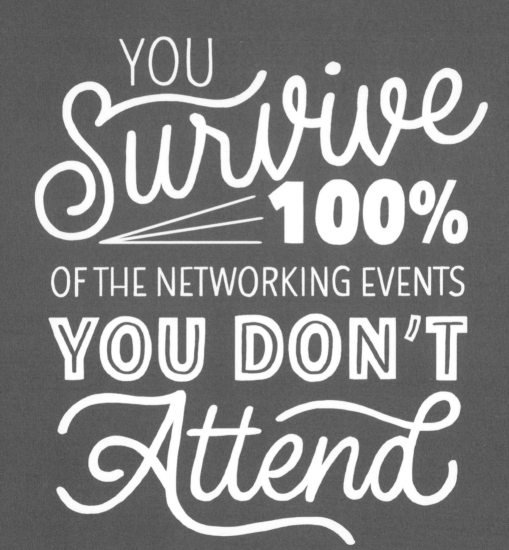

How to Be Harassed Without Hurting His Career

Sexual harassment in the workplace is a serious offense and will not be tolerated, except in cases where the harasser was clearly joking and you need to relax.

In the interest of building a consequence-free environment, here are some tips to avoid reporting sexual harassment and save yourself, your company, and especially your harasser's career a lot of unnecessary suffering.

Understand the cycle of harassment

Some might say being harassed once is enough, but realistically that would bring our industry to a halt. So make sure you remain in the cycle of being harassed at least a few revolutions before considering doing anything about it.

Know who's accountable
for harassment

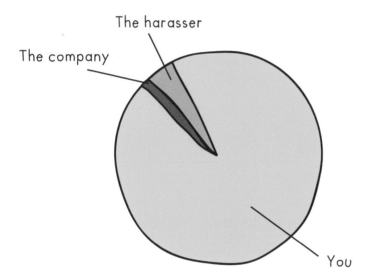

The harasser

The company

You

Accountability is very important to us, specifically, your accountability.

Protect yourself

Protect yourself from harassment by knowing
where to go and where to avoid.

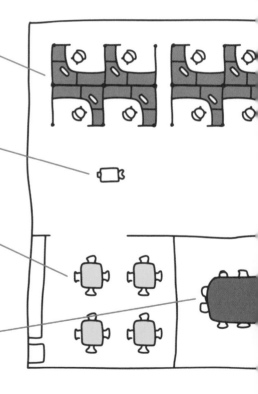

CUBICLES: Avoid staying at
your desk for too long where you
could become the target of
unwanted massages

PRINTER: Try converting the
printer into a standing desk so you
can remain where everyone can
see you

BREAK ROOM: Keep your trips
to the break room speedy so you
don't find yourself cornered in there

CONFERENCE ROOM:
Thankfully, in large conference
rooms you'll usually only experience
microaggressions

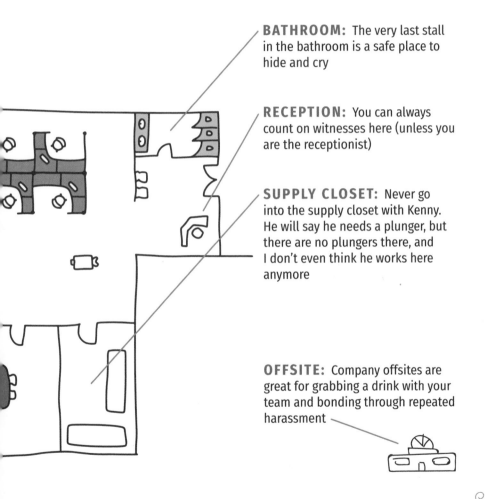

BATHROOM: The very last stall in the bathroom is a safe place to hide and cry

RECEPTION: You can always count on witnesses here (unless you are the receptionist)

SUPPLY CLOSET: Never go into the supply closet with Kenny. He will say he needs a plunger, but there are no plungers there, and I don't even think he works here anymore

OFFSITE: Company offsites are great for grabbing a drink with your team and bonding through repeated harassment

Harassment Survival Kit

Here's a cheat sheet of responses to keep handy for the everyday physical harassment you might experience.

INTENSE EYE CONTACT

If you experience intense eye contact, challenge the harasser to a staring contest, making a fun game out of it, and letting him win quickly so you can leave the room.

TOUCHING CHEEK

Someone may creepily touch your face. The best response here is to jerk your head back while laughing, but beware of whiplash injuries.

SMELLING HAIR

If your hair is smelled or touched without your consent, gently swat the person away while turning your head to the side and laughing.

NECK AND SHOULDERS

Unwanted neck or shoulder massage? Simply cringe your shoulders upward and lean away from the unwanted massage while saying you just got a massage last weekend.

GRABBING ELBOW

If someone tries to lead you by the elbow, take out your phone so you have an excuse to get your elbow out of the way.

BACK SCRATCH

Respond to a back scratch by arching sharply away from the touch while laughing.

PAT ON BUTT

A pat on the butt should be met with light laughter and maybe yelling "Hey!" while swatting the hand away and making a mental note to never be alone with this person.

THIGH GRAZE

If someone grazes your thigh with theirs, start coughing uncontrollably. Say you're definitely coming down with something. Add a slight laugh.

HOLDING HAND

If someone grabs your hand, pull your hand away and laugh while mentioning your always-sweaty palms.

WAIST GRAB

If someone grabs your waist, contort your body away from the hand while pretending to show your coworker a new dance move.

KNEE SQUEEZE

If someone squeezes your knee, remember you have another meeting right now and just get out of there.

FOOTSIE

If someone starts playing footsie under the conference room table, make an excuse about how uncomfortable your new shoes are and shift your position.

Don't be harassed by high performers

There's not much we can do since he's such a high perfomer

One way to save the company a lot of time and money is if you could graciously agree to not be harassed by high performers or employees who are highly regarded. Try to think of the company before letting this happen to you.

Consequences are directly related to job performance

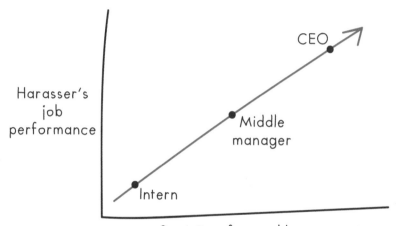

Consider that the higher the performer, the more egregious the harassment will need to be before we barely acknowledge it, then reprimand you for letting it happen.

Was it really harassment?

A lot of times we think we were harassed when we really weren't.
Here are a few examples of harassment vs. not harassment:

HARASSMENT	NOT HARASSMENT
Unwanted touching	Unwanted touching that was harmless and meant to be supportive
Inappropriate nicknames	Inappropriate nicknames that are accurate and/or really funny
Prolonged staring	Prolonged staring when your top is especially bright today
Suggestive emails	Suggestive emails that end with a smiley face

HARASSMENT

Comparing coworkers
to strippers

Spreading rumors about
a coworker

Repeatedly asking for a date

Creepy comments about
body or clothing

Exposing body parts

Demanding sexual favors in
exchange for career advancement

NOT HARASSMENT

Comparing coworkers to
strippers in a low voice so as not
to be heard by said coworkers

Spreading rumors about a
coworker who's probably
going to quit anyway

Repeatedly asking for a
date when you didn't say
"No" forcefully enough

Creepy comments about
body or clothing followed
by an invitation to comment
on his body or clothing

Exposing body parts "by accident"

Demanding sexual favors in
exchange for career advancement
if he's your mentor

Collect evidence, then keep it to yourself

Eye witnesses
Ear witnesses
Other victims

Video
Audio
Emails

Screenshots
Photos
Voice recordings

Instant messages
Documents
Spreadsheets
Affidavits

If you do believe you've been sexually harassed, collect as much evidence as you can. Then, either keep it to yourself, or share it secretly with others. Just be aware that if we do find evidence of you collecting evidence of sexual harassment, you will be reprimanded for collecting that evidence.

Be flexible about making necessary changes

Once you do report harassment, please be flexible about switching positions, desks, offices, projects, teams, companies, and/or careers.

Conclusion

When it comes to sexual harassment, if you have the choice between doing the right thing and being cool, always choose cool. Ask yourself, how can I put my personal safety aside to create a more fun work environment? Finally, if you do report sexual harassment, be prepared to take full responsibility for your harasser's actions. This isn't victim blaming, because you are not a victim, you are a survivor. So it is survivor blaming.

EXERCISE: SEXUAL HARASSMENT LOG

There's nothing wrong with keeping track of when you've been harassed, as long as you do it in a way that absolves your harasser and the company of any wrongdoing. Use this exercise to log the sexual harassment you experience and categorize it as just a joke, all in good fun, or whatever other bullshit excuse they give you.

SEXUAL HARASSMENT

> LOG <

WHAT HAPPENED
Describe the incident then classify
it as just a joke, all in good fun, or
some other excuse they gave you.

	JUST A JOKE	ALL IN GOOD FUN	BULLSHIT

Bonus Tip

PERFORMANCE REVIEW CHEAT SHEET

HARD WORKER = Never finishes anything

GREAT ATTITUDE = Might be on drugs

GOOD COMMUNICATOR = Needs to stop emailing me

CREATIVE PROBLEM SOLVER = Creates a lot of problems

COLLABORATIVE = Gets other people to do his work

RESULTS DRIVEN = Will throw you under the bus

EXCELLENT TIME MANAGEMENT SKILLS = Uses meetings to check email

PASSIONATE = Always interrupting me

DETAIL-ORIENTED = Has no clue what we do here

PUNCTUAL = Leaves every day at 5

Bonus Tip

HONEST MEETING AGENDA

2:00 PM   No one is here

2:02 PM   Someone shows up but leaves again because no one is here

2:06 PM   Everyone is here except the "important person"

2:07 PM   Important person shows up and apologizes for being late, then complains that there's no agenda

2:08–2:15 PM   Try to get the presentation to work

2:16–2:17 PM   Try to get the person dialing in to mute their phone

2:18–2:27 PM   Try to understand the point of this meeting

2:28 PM   Someone shows up asking what he missed

2:29 PM   Important person walks out without explanation

2:30 PM   Meeting adjourned, someone suggests a follow-up

EVERYONE HAS THEIR OWN PATH

Never Compare

YOURSELF TO OTHERS WHO ARE

Younger, Better Looking

Richer, Smarter

AND MORE

AWESOME THAN YOU

Choose Your Own Adventure:
Do You Want to Be Likeable or Successful?

In her book *Dare Mighty Things*, Halee Gray Scott identified the catch-22 for all female leaders: "To succeed, you need to be liked, but to be liked, you need to temper your success."

In this chapter you can explore the choices you're inclined to make and find out if in the end you'll be successful or likeable because unfortunately you can't be both. Are you ready for the adventure of a lifetime but more likely just the next two minutes? Let's go!

There is an open position to lead your team. Do you:

A

Go to your manager and say you'd like to be considered for the role

GO TO PAGE 147

B

Act like you don't want the position even though you really do

GO TO PAGE 148

Your manager thinks a promotion is unlikely but tells you to go for it anyway. Do you:

A

Gather numerous recommendations and write a lengthy, airtight self-evaluation

B

Start to apply but give up halfway through, you probably won't get it anyway

GO TO PAGE 149

GO TO PAGE 148

Jim gets the position and is now your boss. He comes to you often for advice. Do you:

A

Give him great, helpful advice and pick up his slack wherever you can

GO TO PAGE 150

B

Don't help him at all

GO TO PAGE 151

You've been promoted! But your team isn't too happy about it. Do you:

A

Tell them to suck it up

B

Downplay your authority so it doesn't seem like you're really in charge

GO TO PAGE 152

GO TO PAGE 154

You are now basically doing Jim's job for him even though you aren't getting paid more. Do you:

A

Decide to join a different team even though it's at a lower level

GO TO PAGE 154

B

Go to Jim's boss to complain

GO TO PAGE 153

Jim isn't doing such a great job. He is ousted and you are offered his position. Do you:

A

Take the position, and be seen as the reason Jim leaves the company

GO TO PAGE 155

B

Refuse the position to avoid rocking the boat

GO TO PAGE 154

One particular member of your team undermines you at every turn and clearly wants your job. Do you:

A

Get rid of him

GO TO PAGE 155

B

Take a leave of absence, letting this person nab your job

GO TO PAGE 154

Your boss's boss doesn't want to lose you so you get a pay increase. Jim now has it out for you. Do you:

A

Decide to join a different team at a higher level

GO TO PAGE 155

B

Back off and let Jim take all the credit for your work

GO TO PAGE 154

You are likeable!

You've preserved personal relationships at the expense of your career and now you can safely say you have lots of friends to help you move into a more affordable apartment.

You are successful!

You've worked hard to get ahead and should be proud of your success, even if it means no one talks to you at lunch or ever tells you what they really think.

Conclusion

You may go through different stages of being more successful than likeable or more likeable than successful or neither likeable nor successful. But one day you'll wake up and you won't care about being either and that's the day you'll be the most successful and most likeable person, at least to yourself.

EXERCISE: EXISTENTIAL ORG CHART

One way to keep your hunger for power in check is to remind yourself about all the things that are more important than what you want, such as being liked, not offending anyone, your need to appear more attractive to insecure men, etc. Write them down in this existential org chart.

EXISTENTIAL

ORG CHART

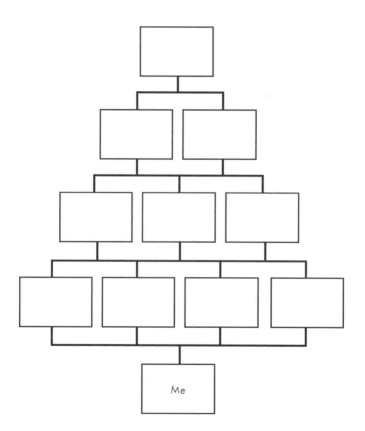

START EACH DAY
WITH A
Positive
Thought
SUCH AS
I'm going back to
BED NOW

CHAPTER 10: ALLIES

Men's Achievement Stickers

In our gentle request for equal rights, we must find allies. And for non-threatening women, the best path to building those allies is positive reinforcement. This means you should avoid pointing out all the brain-dead, dumbass shit things men do and instead lavish them with praise for what they're doing right. Yes, even if that thing they're doing right is just basic human decency.

Because let's face it ladies, we need to take what we can get. So celebrate basic human decency like there's no tomorrow with these achievement stickers for men.

TALKED FOR LESS THAN **95%** OF THE MEETING

TREATED A WOMAN LIKE A HUMAN

SAID

Well, actually

ONLY ONCE

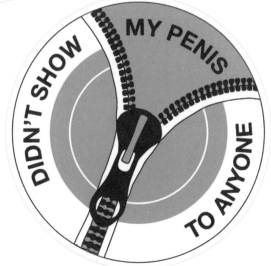

DIDN'T SHOW MY PENIS TO ANYONE

SURVIVED A MAN-COLD

CALLED OUT A JERK FOR BEING A JERK

DIDN'T SUGGEST **STRIP CLUB** FOR THE COMPANY OFFSITE

KEPT THERMOSTAT ABOVE

62° F

CONSIDERED *the* IDEA *of the* POSSIBILITY *of the* EXISTENCE *of* SEXISM

MADE ONE LESS EXCUSE FOR MY TRASH FRIEND

KEPT HIGH FIVES TO A MINIMUM

STOPPED MYSELF WHILE EXPLAINING SOMETHING I DIDN'T UNDERSTAND

WAITED AN EXTRA MINUTE BEFORE INTERRUPTING FEMALE COWORKER

DIDN'T REFER TO WATCHING MY KIDS AS "BABYSITTING"

LET
Someone
Else
HAVE THE LAST WORD

WONDERED IF MAYBE...
THIS WASN'T ABOUT ME?

Conclusion

If you find a man who has the distinct honor of receiving all of these stickers, beware, he might be a woman. Or a robot. Or an alien.

EXERCISE: BEST COMPLIMENTS TRACKER

Men always give the best compliments don't they? Use this log to keep track of all your favorites and which ones make you feel the most special.

BEST COMPLIMENTS

TRACKER

Wow, you don't LOOK like an engineer!

Pretty AND smart!

A girl with a brain!

We need more females like you!

You're too pretty for this job!

That's so great you balance work with kids!

Bonus Tip

EMAIL BINGO

"I hope this finds you well"	"Sorry for the delay"	"I'm just seeing this now"	"Is this still needed?"	"Bump"
"Happy *day of the week*"	The weather	ALL CAPS	Bold words	Forgot attachment
Passive-aggressive comment	Unnecessary emojis	FREE: Auto-responder	"Quick question"	"Quick update"
"Just checking in"	"Just following up"	"Would a phone call be better?"	"Thanks in advance"	"Please don't reply all"
"Best"	"Cheers"	"Warm regards"	"Sent from my iPhone"	Disclaimer longer than email itself

Bonus Tip

ABILITY to FOCUS OVER TIME

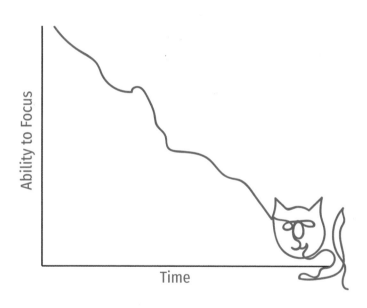

YOUR IMPOSTER SYNDROME WILL NEVER Be good enough

CHAPTER 11: ENTREPRENEURSHIP

The Perfect Pitch Deck for the Kickass Lady Boss

As a female entrepreneur, you've unfortunately already exceeded the threatening threshold for non-threatening women. Although you can't escape the threatening label now, you can mitigate some of the ill effects by thinking ahead and keeping in mind all of the double standards you'll be subjected to as a woman who runs her own company.

To head off some of these inane situations, make sure your pitch deck is airtight. Any pitch deck you create should include these ten slides.

ABOUT the FOUNDER

Marlene Stevens, Mompreneur

One great way to remove the sting of being a powerful woman is to give yourself a cute, feminine title that reminds investors that yes, you are a leader, but you are also still a woman. Some options are:

- Girl Boss
- Lady Boss
- She-EO
- Business Mogulette

- Parentrepreneur
- Mompreneur
- Womantrepreneur
- Estrogentreprenuer

ABOUT MY WHITE MALE COFOUNDER

Ryan Archibald, Male Cofounder
(a white man)

Investors follow patterns when trying to figure out what to invest in, and one of those patterns is that most successful CEOs are white men. Inventing a fake white male cofounder will match the pattern and bring legitimacy to your business idea.* And, beyond the pitch meeting, you can use your fake founder for business communications when you'd like to actually get a response to your email.

*See Penelope Gazin and Kate Dwyer of Witchsy.

MY PRODUCT:
THE PERFECT SHIRT for
SHORT, STOCKY, STYLELESS MEN

Make sure your product is something your potential investors could personally see themselves using, or else they won't be able to see any value in it whatsoever. Even though women are half of the population, remember, anything targeting them is considered a niche market.

If your product is not for men, then make sure it's a product your potential investors could see their mom, girlfriend, wife, secretary, or mistress using. Bonus points if you are able to interview any of these women and get them to endorse your product before the meeting, saving your investor some time when they inevitably feel the need to consult with them.

Since your male cofounder is imaginary and therefore not with you, you won't be able to say things off the cuff without backing up every word with data. Overload your potential investors with so much data they'll be exasperated trying to catch you off guard on anything.

> ### THIS SLIDE
> ### INTENTIONALLY LEFT BLANK
> ### to GIVE YOU TIME to
> ### EXPLAIN MY BUSINESS
> ### to ME

However, be prepared to listen to them explain your business to you, completely ignoring all the data you just presented.

INVESTMENT: $250,000

$125,000: eCommerce backend and app

$50,000: Personnel

$25,000: Marketing

$20,000: Office space and equipment

$15,000: Recruiting

$10,000: Sales channel

$4,000: Fulfillment

$1,000: Storage

Although a male founder can walk in and ask for 3 million dollars to spend on "swag, or whatever," don't expect the same trust. Make sure to detail exactly how you will spend every last penny of the money you're asking for, and definitely don't include swag.

MORE ABOUT ME

I am married

I rent, I do not own

Yes, my husband has a real job

Yes, this is my full-time thing

I am half Portuguese and half Jewish

I do not have an accent

Thank you, I got this dress at Macy's

My child goes to Midland Middle School

Be prepared to field nonrelevant questions about your background, your personal history, your appearance, your husband, your kids, your social life, and your dog. And make sure you get your fake laugh ready for all those typical male jokes you will hear over and over and over again.

SAFE FOR LUNCH and DINNER MEETINGS

Investors are often wary of going to lunch, dinner, or drinks with a female founder, even though they would happily do the same with their male founders. To put their minds at ease about being a sexual harassment risk, offer to attend out-of-office meetings in a plastic bubble.

YOUR PORTFOLIO

Investors are always looking for ways to make it seem like they care about diversity, so give them the opportunity to feature you on their website in exchange for meeting with you once a quarter and providing useless advice. This lets them have the visibility of working with diverse founders without having to actually invest in your company—a great selling point.

Conclusion

Anticipating exactly what your investors want will make their decision to invest in you much easier. And, if you're one step ahead of your investors, you'll be that much closer to being forty-nine steps behind their male founders.

EXERCISE: *SPORTS METAPHOR WORKSHEET*

If you're in any male-dominated business environment, chances are you're going to hear a lot of sports metaphors. Make sure you keep your game sharp and know where these popular phrases come from. And don't even think about using any non-sports metaphors men may not understand; this will gravely upset them.

SPORTS METAPHOR

WORKSHEET

Skate to where the puck's going to be

In your wheelhouse

Full-court press

The ball's in their court

Down for the count

Under the wire

Knock it out of the park

Slam dunk

Swing for the fences

Par for the course

Go to the mat

No holds barred

Call an audible

Move the goal posts

Monday-morning quarterback

Pulling a Rosie Ruiz

Hockey

Football

Baseball

Horse racing

Golf

Running

Wrestling

Tennis

Basketball

Boxing

Soccer

Bonus Tip

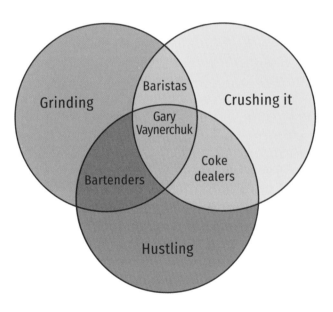

Bonus Tip

TODDLER vs. CEO

 Blurts out random opinions which are then treated as gold

 Uses special made-up words

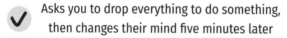 Asks you to drop everything to do something, then changes their mind five minutes later

Throws a tantrum if they don't get what they want

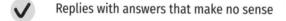 Replies with answers that make no sense

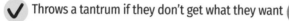 Gets completely obsessed with the most insignificant things

 Collects, then quickly discards, expensive toys

Interrupts every conversation to share their own tangentially related thoughts

 Loves when you take vacation

REWARD YOURSELF FOR ONLY Eating HALF THE COOKIE By eating the OTHER HALF OF THE COOKIE

CHAPTER 12: SELF-CARE

How to Relax While Still Completely Stressing Yourself Out

Me time. Ever heard of it? Me either. It doesn't exist. But we try to make it exist anyway, and we go through all kinds of effort to force ourselves to relax even though just the thought of relaxing is already too stressful to bear.

Here are a few great ways to relax while still doing what you're supposed to be doing, which is worrying about what you should be doing instead.

SELF-CARE IDEA #1

Get acupuncture while wondering if it'd be just as effective for you to buy the pins and do it yourself

GREAT FOR:

When a male coworker who started after you gets promoted before you

Meditate while replaying yesterday's disaster presentation over and over again in your head

Why did I
keep saying
"actually"

GREAT FOR:

When you caught your boss falling asleep during your presentation

SELF-CARE IDEA #3

Stay home from work to recharge and decompress, then end up cleaning your entire house

I'm going to scrub this spot forever

GREAT FOR:

When your coworker writes a manifesto about how women aren't biologically suited for their jobs

SELF-CARE IDEA #4

Rock back and forth in a fetal position and imagine what would happen if a coworker saw you like this

I would just tell them this is part of my improv class

GREAT FOR:

When a coworker derails your meeting and now you're too scared to schedule a new meeting to discuss what the first meeting was supposed to be about

SELF-CARE IDEA #5

Gather all your blankets and pillows and sit on your couch with a cup of tea you never drink

Dammit this tea is already cold

GREAT FOR:

When you realize at this rate you won't be able to retire until you're ninety

SELF-CARE IDEA #6

Doodle in an adult coloring book and think of what an amazing career you could've had as an artist

GREAT FOR:

When your mentor won't call you back

Decide to spend one extra minute in the shower then waste it feeling guilty about wasting water

I'm so sorry environment

GREAT FOR:

When you stayed up all night writing an email you ultimately decided not to send

SELF-CARE IDEA #8

Eat a whole bowl of pasta and savor every bite while also counting the calories in every bite

562, 662...

762, 862, 962..

GREAT FOR:

When you come across a photo of you from ten years ago and you have no idea what you were doing with your life

Look at pictures of kittens online, then baby otters, then baby elephants, then puppies, then kittens again

Awwww

GREAT FOR:

When you've just spent six hours online comparing yourself to a younger, more successful woman

Quit your job, cut your hair, change your name, and take a one-way trip to Greece

GREAT FOR:

When you're over it

Conclusion

One thought that calms me is that, no matter which self-care routine I choose, all the things I was worrying about before will still be there when I'm done.

EXERCISE: DAILY APOLOGY CHECKLIST

Apologizing for everything just feels good, doesn't it? You can absolutely never apologize too much. Use this checklist to help you keep track of all the things you may not yet have apologized for today.

DAILY APOLOGY

CHECKLIST

I'M SORRY FOR . . .

- [ ] Responding too late
- [ ] Responding too early
- [ ] Having my headphones on
- [ ] Being interrupted
- [ ] Staring at the bagels
- [ ] Speaking too softly
- [ ] Speaking at all
- [ ] Tripping on a rock (to the rock)
- [ ] Sharing too much
- [ ] Not sharing enough
- [ ] Enjoying food too much
- [ ] Asking a question
- [ ] Being misled
- [ ] Not liking my food
- [ ] Wanting something different
- [ ] Someone taking my seat

- [ ] Saying I'm sorry
- [ ] Asking to be paid
- [ ] Being bumped into
- [ ] Sitting in this chair
- [ ] Taking up space
- [ ] Needing help
- [ ] Offering to help
- [ ] My shoes being loud
- [ ] Going too fast
- [ ] Going too slow
- [ ] Swallowing too loudly
- [ ] Knowing what I'm doing
- [ ] Someone else's mistake
- [ ] Being proud of myself
- [ ] Sharing my thoughts
- [ ] Being successful

Bonus Tip

FRIDAY

SUNDAY

Bonus Tip

SUNDAYS

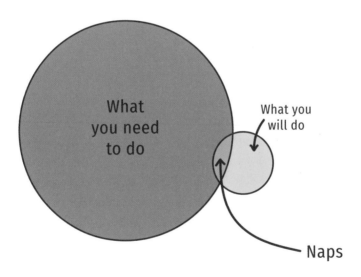

Be
Threatening

When I told men the title of this book, they responded in one of three ways:

1. Men whose feelings were genuinely hurt by the title bristled at the name. They felt it was sexist, abrasive, confrontational, and wrong. They felt attacked. How audacious it was for me to expect that anything I did would penetrate their impenetrable fortress devoid of emotion! These men would never and could never be intimidated by a successful woman and to suggest otherwise was downright preposterous.

I'd like to take the opportunity to apologize to these men for being so threatening in my suggestion that men could feel threatened by me.

2. Men whose feelings were also genuinely hurt, but who didn't want to show it, simply got quiet or pensive and changed the subject. They knew at the outset this book wasn't one they'd ever read because it hurt their feelings in a way they couldn't admit, even to themselves.

I apologize to those men as well, for forcing them to face their uncomfortable relationship with threatening women.

3. On the other hand, men whose feelings were genuinely not hurt laughed when they heard the title. Their laughter was followed by a knowing nod or a tell-me-more grin. And not only that, but they wanted to read the book too, even with such an offensive title! They would read my book, I imagined, just like I had read all those books not explicitly written for men but clearly written for men.

Although they don't need it, I'd still like to apologize to these men for having to deal with the other two types of men.

But do you want to know the craziest part of all of this?

I set out to write a book for women but ended up deathly afraid of what men would think, imagining every possible scenario.

With all these imaginary scenarios involving imaginary men, I had little room in my head for anything else.

Which was, ultimately, the reason for the book in the first place.

This book is not for men. And the title has little to do with how we make men feel. Instead, it's about how we think we make men feel and how we are consumed by trying to make them feel a certain way or avoid feeling a certain way, as if that should be our number one concern.

So how do you be successful without hurting men's feelings? You don't. You be successful whether men's feelings are hurt or not, because really that's up to them, not you.

Maybe they're secure, maybe they're not. Maybe they're sexist assholes, maybe they're not. Maybe they're going to get in your way on your path to your own success and maybe they already have.

But more rules on how we should change in order to better deal with their issues ain't gonna help us, honey.

What will help us is more of us. A lot more of us. Everywhere. So get out there! And be as threatening or as non-threatening as you want.

Special Thanks

To write a book that was hopefully funny but could also make people want to throw it across the room, I relied on the support of very many people.

First off, thank you to my photo models for bringing so much realism to the ridiculous situations I put them in: Nikki Chase, Emily Browning, Heather Young, Hilary Hesse, Emily Corbo, Jason Kyle, Allan Lazo, Christian Baxter, and Alex Garcia.

Thank you to my agent, Susan Raihofer, who told me to trust my gut when I called her halfway through writing the initial concept with the sinking feeling that I was writing the wrong book. Thank you for thinking through all the things I don't have the patience for, for always being honest with me, and most of all for getting that three-book deal, without which these pages probably would never have existed. You knew I could do it but I sure as hell didn't!

To my editor Patty Rice for being even more patient with this book than the last, which I didn't think was possible, and having an impeccable eye for details I always miss. Thank you also to Kirsty Melville for knowing I needed more time several months before I did.

Thank you to my scrappy cadre of early readers and beta testers: Antonella, Tamara O., Molly S., Amber, Susan, Todd, Karen, Matt, Rob, Tia, Tamara W., Michaela, PeiPei, Beth, Brenda, Tam, Stacy, Irving, Christina, Katie, Ragan, Nicole, Molly J., Cianti, Laura, Wayne, Abla, Joe, Laura, and Heather. This book wouldn't exist without you.

And of course, Lance and Jennifer Cooper, Rachael Cooper, Charmaine Cooper, Lance and Susie Cooper, and every other Cooper who made this Cooper possible.

Finally, thank you to my husband, partner, and best friend, Jeff. You are definitely one of the top twenty people I've ever met in 2012.

Andrews McMeel Publishing
a division of Andrews McMeel Universal
1130 Walnut Street, Kansas City, Missouri 64106

www.andrewsmcmeel.com

18 19 20 21 22 SDB 10 9 8 7 6 5 4 3 2 1

ISBN: 978-1-4494-7607-6

Library of Congress Control Number: 2018941651

Editor: Patty Rice
Designer/Art Director: Diane Marsh
Production Editor: Dave Shaw
Production Manager: Tamara Haus
Cover and additional design by Dina Rodriguez
Cover illustration based on photograph by Scott R. Kline

ATTENTION: SCHOOLS AND BUSINESSES
Andrews McMeel books are available at quantity discounts with bulk purchase for educational, business, or sales promotional use. For information, please e-mail the Andrews McMeel Publishing Special Sales Department: specialsales@amuniversal.com.

MUSTACHES

for NON-THREATENING WOMEN

Stickers not intended for children.